How To Treat A Woman

John Joseph

...pectations. Jus' Sayin. Mom is a Kappa.

Hard ta please.

Introduction

"Have you ever seen a woman so beautiful that you thought if you could only have her, you'd treat her so well and you'd be totally in love? The woman you're with now is the one you need to impress. Most think that you capture a woman's heart only once. But quite to the contrary, you must love her enough to try to make her fall in love with you EVERY single day! You should always treat her as if you're trying to win her love for the very first time. No matter how many years have passed, never take her for granted".

This post seems nice and sweet. Right? It was actually written with a bit of anger attached to it. Let me explain. I have always had friends venting to me about their relationships. Everyone tells me what they are happy about, what they are unhappy about, what they need him/her to do, etc. I'm not sure why. I just seem to attract that. I must be a good listener. :)

One such friend was an absolutely beautiful woman. Her boyfriend was not treating her well to say the least. He neglected her, he lied to her and he cheated on her. This amazed me to no end and it made me think. "I am 100 percent certain that he was not behaving like this when he was trying to win her love. Why is he acting like this now?" She was faithful to him no matter what he did or what she heard.

This upset me terribly and made me realize that some people think that once you win somebody over, you are on easy street. As I looked around at other relationships, I started questioning if this was actually true or not. It certainly appeared that way. The older the relationships were, the less effort went in to them.

This was backwards because the beginnings of relationships are easy and it takes a little more work as you move forward. I also believe that there are vital stages and crucial moments in relationships. If you are not aware of them, the relationship can take bad turns. Or what usually happens is that it goes on a slow and steady decline. There are some things you can never lose sight of to make a healthy relationship.

If you are ready, I will take you on a journey starting from the first date to late in the relationship. I am going to talk about some problem areas that I have experienced and state some concepts that have helped me finally build a strong relationship. Some of these will be explained with stories that you will find towards the end. I hope you enjoy. :)

The First Date

Have you ever seen a woman so beautiful that you thought if you could only have her, you'd treat her so well and you'd be totally in love? What if you were lucky enough to get a date with her? What would you do?

When I first started dating, I was always nervous on the first date. One of the main reasons was that I had NO clue what to do! I always wondered where to go on the date, if I should bring flowers, open her car door, close her car door, always let her go first, pull out her chair before she sits down, etc, etc, etc. I learned pretty quickly that even if I thought I did everything perfectly, I could blow it in other ways.

One way I found to blow it before the date even started was to sit on the phone with her asking her what she wanted to do. I had been guilty of that, so I figured out that I needed to talk about going to a specific restaurant or to see a specific movie. Not, to simply go to dinner and/or to the movies. Then at least I had some semblance of a plan.

I definitely didn't want to ruin everything by forgetting to do something simple. My other worry was that not everyone likes the same things on dates, so how would I know what to do and what not to do. I decided that it was best for me to just take everything as it comes. I would do one thing that was always set in stone. Open all doors for her and let her go first. My goal was to not let her touch one doorknob or handle.

One of my biggest problems was always the car door. This was because I was unsure if this was what she wanted and it is just so obvious that you are going to do this when you walk over to her side. This made me nervous. I was so clueless that I would leave something on the passenger seat and act like I had to open the door to move it for her. Then since I was there anyway, I would close the door behind her. If I could do this the first time, this seemed to break the ice for the rest of the night. This was BAD! It pretty much negated that action and she was never fooled by it. So, I found out that it is best to just do it and mean it!

Another thing this does is it sets the tone of the date, and you don't want to lose her attention before you get to what really matters. The purpose or goal of the date! If you are truly thinking long term, what is it? To get acquainted? To start the beginning of the screening process? To have fun? Sure! We can list much more. But there is something that needs to happen in order for this date to be called a success. It has nothing to do with where you went, what you did or the dating etiquette that you followed.

What needs to happen is an event, a moment, a connection. You need a unique situation that causes you to connect with her on a deeper level. This is NOT a kiss, or a touch or sex. It's that brief moment that you connect on a mental, emotional and spiritual level all at once. Do you know this moment? It's that split second when both of you know that something just happened and you can see it in her eyes. Your knees may get weak and you may get goose bumps. Many things can set this off but it cannot be forced! You have to find it, not create it.

Go experience something that is new to both of you. A unique moment that when you think of that time and place, you think of her and ONLY her! This will be the first anchor in the relationship. So make it good!

Dating

When we are dating, what are we really doing? From a current perspective, you may think that it's just getting to know someone better, testing to see if they are the right one or even some more shallow reasons. But, being in a long term relationship and looking back you will see that what you were really doing is creating a collection of special moments with that person. So, realize this from the very start. Everything you are doing is going to have a great impact on how beautiful your relationship can be.

Once I was past the first date, I always thought that this was a big step that she has allowed me to take. At this point, I felt that the least I could do was to keep tabs on my feelings about her. Meaning that I would search my feelings and come to terms on how far I saw this going with her. Sometimes I needed a little time. But, if I knew I did not see it going anywhere, it was the time to let her know.

Finally in one of my relationships, I felt that there was a good chance that I had found the one! I wanted to make all of my time with her meaningful. I continued to look for these special connections together. This mindset opened my eyes to settings that helped make some of the special moments happen. I started to automatically look for nice and romantic atmospheres. Over dinner, I looked deeply into her eyes. I held her hand all the time. I was saying nice things more often. I found myself wanting to learn everything about her. She told me everything she liked and what things moved her.

She told me the answers to the questions I had about her before the very first date. I knew that it was very important to remember the details. For example, she told me early on that she liked flowers. So, I needed to find out what type of flowers, what color, where and how often she liked to receive them. I had a bad memory. So as soon as I got a chance, I wrote everything down and kept it in a safe place.

It worked like a charm. I just had to simply pay attention and the things that I previously had so many challenges with, started to come naturally. Is this how women always know exactly the right thing to do for men on special occasions? Because when we say that we like something, they make a note of it? The important thing for me was that I started paying more attention and this was becoming effortless.

As time went on, these special moments seemed to be like links in a chain that I was welding together. This is what relationships are built upon. So, here I was as all of those moments got linked together. I knew that in one of those moments, if it was meant to be, we were going to fall in love. Of course I did not know the exact moment this was for her, but I knew which moment it was for me.

We like to think it was at the exact same time. How romantic is it to think you fell in love with each other at the very same moment? It's never really talked about, but it is more than romantic. It's powerful!

Another thing that actually turned out to be pretty vital to my relationship was remembering the little moments. Women have great memories when it comes to ALL of your experiences together. Some men do not. But at some point down the road, she is going to ask you "remember when we were at ____

and this happened?" Wasn't that fun? She is asking you this because something very meaningful happened there and she wants to make sure that connection is still there.

If you do not remember it, you are going to be in trouble. She may actually start to re-evaluate things if this happens multiple times. Relationships have ended due to this. Think about it. If you have a meaningful experience with someone where you and that person connected and that person forgets about it, wouldn't you feel alone? These are the moments that are building your relationship. Remember and cherish every moment!

Don't Let It Stagnate

Previously when I had been dating someone for a while, it seemed that there was a point in the relationship that everything seemed to slow down. This was usually somewhere within the 6-12 month area. This is when many people think that the excitement wears off and if they've made it through that part, they just get complacent. Of course others take this as the time to move on.

Sometimes, you can get caught up in doing the same things over and over again. Have you ever ordered pizza together and you had pizza and wine while watching a movie on a Friday night? That's the best. Isn't it? The first time you may light a bunch of candles and sit together watching as the candlelight shimmers off of the wine glasses.

You start feeling really good and the night is just amazing. Somehow this becomes an every Friday or Saturday night event. In time, it changes. There are no candles anymore, all the lights are on and you look at it as having plain old pizza and cheap wine while you watch reruns on TV.

We have all heard a woman say: "He just doesn't know what he wants"? OR worse. She actually tells her man that HE just doesn't know what he wants? Usually, they say this when the man has gotten complacent and the relationship is not progressing. The crazy thing about this is that this is usually EXACTLY what he does want. He is happy where things are. In my experience, this was never acceptable. So, what do we do? Change things up a little. Do not get in the routine of just sitting at home doing the same old thing. Being at home is fine sometimes, but do different things. Men also need a little push most of the time.

I would have relationships where it seemed like both of us were just tolerating each other. This just didn't seem right. I didn't want to just tolerate someone. So, I just ended up having one 6-month relationship after another so I could always have that new relationship feeling. I didn't have to do this. I could have kept the excitement going forever. I just didn't realize it.

I decided to keep working on finding new and unique special moments with her and it was always exciting. I just kept linking together those special moments! We did the little things that mattered to each other. When the excitement felt like it was starting to wear off, we built more special moments. This is part of the "work" they talk about in order for a relationship to be successful. I found that it was not too much work at all. It was actually very fun!

Step It Up

Something else that women need is Progress! A sign of moving forward is very important. This was hard for me and painful at times. I imagine most men struggle with this. I was always happy and content with the relationship staying right where it was. I didn't even think about how it would progress until she would bring it up. I felt it was so easy to just go with the flow and it felt like work to move forward. But most women do not take this lightly yet it seems to be a comfort zone for men.

A friend of mine once showed me a list she had made. It had specific things that her man needed to do by a specific day/year. It included things like saying I Love You, making a definite commitment, meeting his family, going on a trip together, giving them a key to their place, plans to live together, proposing to them (with a date). All of this was an ongoing conversation until all of the above were accomplished! The amazing thing was that all of these goals happened pretty close to the timeframe she set for them.

When I looked at this I realized that all of these things are the makings of special moments. You need to make all of these things fun and powerful. You are building the future of your relationship here, and these are the building blocks. You control if they are strong or weak.

I actually made a list of all of these points of progress for my own relationship. I knew I was not going to go and accomplish all of them right away. But, I kept referring to them and kept asking myself if they were all realistically in our future. If not, I had to figure out why not? Then talk to her about it. I actually found that she was in the same place that I was on a lot of the progress points. We simply had to talk more specifically and then decide what our goals were together.

This point was a crucial point. Sometimes it's hard to get through when you are not exactly on the same page. So you need to always remember my original question: "Have you ever seen a woman so beautiful that you thought if you could only have her, you'd treat her so well and you'd be totally in love?" This seems to be forgotten later in relationships, which is nothing short of a crime.

Later Years

Later in relationships and marriages, things seem to change so much that the relationship is not even recognizable. Sometimes, the passion goes away and everything comes to a complete stop! You get these problems that seem to show up later in relationships. A lot of these same issues may have always been there, but they are now coming to the surface having a detrimental effect your relationship.

There are couples that live on opposite sides of the house. They don't even talk throughout the day. They even sleep in different rooms. There is no longer a relationship.

What makes this happen? How do you avoid this?

I know this sounds a little repetitive at this point. But if this is happening, you need more, up to date, special moments. Your links are either too weak, or they have weakened over time. You need to make her more important than any problem that may come up.

Go back and remember your first date and everything you did to try to win her over. I don't care how many years into it you are. Follow the same plan. It is AMAZING what this can do! Fall in LOVE all over again!

This is being restated at the end to drive home an important point.

Somehow, this seems more powerful in the beginning of a relationship. Just like love, this should become more powerful with time.

"Have you ever seen a woman so beautiful that you thought if you could only have her, you'd treat her so well and you'd be totally in love? The woman you're with now is the one you need to impress. Most think you capture a woman's heart once. But quite to the contrary, you must love her enough to try to make her fall in love with you EVERY single day! You should always treat her as if you're trying to win her love for the very first time. No matter how many years have passed, never take her for granted".

Four Short Stories

Our First Trip Together

Cuddling

And So We Danced

Feel The Love On Valentine's Day

Our First Trip Together

Before we were together, we would flirtatiously talk about going away together. It was just talk, but it would instill such strong thoughts. Talking about this with someone you like fills your mind with such images that are so vivid and grand. You picture what you might do together, how you would experience things and what you can learn from each other. In your mind, everything is perfect.

In the following months, we started dating. The plans for a weekend trip naturally started to take form. Living close to one of the theme park capitals of the world, it was easy just to take off and spend the weekend there. I slowly came to the realization that this was not the carefree, dream trip that we had imagined. This was actually a crucial point in our relationship. Most think that you will know if the relationship can work after you go on your first trip together. It's treated as a test to see how much you can "tolerate" the other person. There were so many things that we were going to learn about each other. I was afraid that we would not be able to handle it.

Not even 45 miles down the road our first disagreement started. I started wondering if this trip was doomed from the start. Are we going to have a good time? Will

SHE have a good time? Is she going to be thinking about things back home while we are far away together? Will she wish she were there? Should I just turn around now? Of course not! We are going to one of the most fun places in the world. There is no way we can fail.

When we visited the parks, all we were concerned about was what to ride next, what shows to see, where to eat lunch. Literally rushing from one attraction to the next. By the time we got to the room, we were exhausted. We knew we still had to go eat dinner and we were very irritable. I just wanted to lie down, but she wanted to go eat in this beautiful restaurant we had previously discovered. Another argument was about to break out. I had to think for a moment to regain my senses. I assured her that we will eat soon, but I asked her to just rest with me for a few minutes. We were obviously VERY tired. I had to turn the lights off. Just for a few minutes. She laid down with her head on my chest and my arm around her. It was Dark. The only sound was the blowing of the air conditioner.

Just before we drifted to sleep, I was thinking about the day we just shared. We rushed through everything trying to take it all in. Not once did we take an opportunity to look over the beautiful scenes and experience them as one. To point out the little beautiful things would have

allowed us to savor the moments.
This was a trip with built in special
moments just there waiting to
happen!

We were ignoring the
opportunities to take each other in. I
was on the verge of wanting a
second chance at that day. But fate,
it seems, is never without purpose.
The missing "moment" that I
regretted not having, was
happening now. It was being
together resting and the realization
of how we can have done better by
including each other.

After our little nap, I
mentioned nothing of my thoughts.
I wanted to turn them into action.
There was still tension in the air.

Walking over to the restaurant we walked over this beautiful wooden bridge that had a waterfall right along the side of it. Taking her by the hand, I turned her to face me. I held a coin up at eye level and looked her in the eye as to ask her if she wanted to make a wish. Her answer was a stern "NO" obviously thinking that was childish. However, she became more playful she looked away but she still had my hand. All the stress of the day seemed to have drained away.

Over dinner, our eyes reconnected as they were by the waterfall. We began to notice all of the little things that we were missing. For the rest of the trip, we always looked into each other's eyes when something was happening. As if we wanted each other's reaction so we could share it. It is one thing to experience life with someone at your side. But, always make sure you are connected on the same level. You can experience things "as ONE".

Cuddling

Cuddling is very underrated. You can do A lot with cuddling. But, A man will say he wants to cuddle when he just wants sex. Since everyone probably doesn't like the same thing, there is probably not one right way to cuddle. I will tell you a little story. So, if it's early, get your coffee. If it's late, get a glass of wine and enjoy this.

Years ago, a girl I know called me one night because she was bored. She wanted to hang out, but she made it clear that she was not there for sex. She explained that she is not the kind of girl, etc. I really knew this already because she was a very proper girl with strong family values. I assured her that I am aware of that and not to worry about anything.

At around 8:00pm, she came over. We talked for around an hour and she all of a sudden wanted to watch a movie. So, I picked a good movie out of my collection. I also opened a bottle of wine. I love red wine especially when I'm home on a weekend night. So, of course I offered some to her and she accepted. I want to make clear that this is all she had. She made it a point to not drink too much.

So there we were sipping wine, watching a movie and talking. I was on the floor keeping my distance so she wouldn't think I was trying anything. I like sitting on the floor next to my coffee table anyway.

As the night went on, she seemed to look at me like "what am I doing on the floor?" She told me to come sit on the couch with her. Remembering my assurance to her, I made it a point to be as good as possible.

Eventually, she wanted to lay down to watch TV and she allowed me to lay down next to her on the couch. She was very comfortable and she pulled my arm over her. Basically, we were in a spooning kind of position. After a while, she wasn't even watching the movie anymore. Her eyes were closed and she looked content. We ended up going to the bedroom to get more comfortable.

Wanting a little more contact, but not wanting to violate any rules that have been established, I lightly place my hand on her arm. She didn't move away, so I was thinking that this was okay. I timidly started to, ever so slightly, move my hand. Very slowly and only moving about an inch back and forth. This was Very light to the touch. She allowed this to take place, so I continued. I expanded the area on her arm that I was lightly stroking until she moved her arm away and my hand was resting on her side. I then started moving my hand in the same manner on her side. Her shirt was short, so I was able to start doing this on her skin.

It seemed that whenever I touched her a little bit outside of the original area, she got chills and goose bumps. I slowly expanded the area I was delicately stroking. Her reactions grew stronger when I drifted towards her stomach or towards her leg flirting with her waistline.

I was doing all of this very subtly and she liked it. I figured she liked it because her body started to move in a way that was showing me where to touch next. We were still in the same position. Only now both of my arms were around her. While I was holding her with both of my arms, both of my hands were now moving slowly over her body. I would never touch any "forbidden" areas. But, when I got close to them, her body would just tremble with a quick yet quiet heavy breath.

Before we fell asleep, I pulled her whole body into mine tightly. You know it's right when your bodies just fit together. Almost like a puzzle. We would take naps through the night and wake up together, and this would start all over again.

Now I was holding her with both arms and she was facing me. It was very dark, but I could still look into her eyes and see her looking back. She then did something surprising. She got on top of me as if she just wanted to feel how I felt and she gave me a kiss.

Then she laid back down with her head on my chest. We fell asleep again. When the sun came up, I did not want to let go of her. I knew I had to get up, so I moved a little and she woke up and looked at the clock. It was dark in the room with sunlight dripping in through the edges of the blinds.

As I got up, I told her that I had to get ready. I walked to her side and gave her a kiss, and she forcefully took my hand and pulled me back under the covers!

Hope you liked it! :)

And So We Danced

A long time ago when I was young and VERY shy, I was at a function. It was the kind of event that's usually in a ballroom and there is assigned seating. Maybe a wedding, but I was alone. I remember that much. I also remember the low lighting and soft music playing. Everything that the light, from the small dim lamps, could not reach was illuminated by only candles. The soft music matched this mood and it came from a small jazz trio hidden away in the corner.

I was up walking around and made my way back to my table. Just before I reached to pull my chair out. A girl stopped me. I was stunned for a moment by her beauty. She asked me to dance. I was not much of a dancer, but the song that was playing was slow. So, I agreed and she pulled me by the arm through the maze of tables.

We stopped at the dancing area and just looked at each other for a moment. Still stunned by her, I felt a sense of numbness. The kind where you don't know if your knees are going to give out and you feel little control over your legs and feet. So, We danced VERY slowly. She had these dark eyes that attracted every little bit of candlelight from the tables. It had this shimmering effect and I just stared into them. Feeling as if I was truly looking deeper within her, I became lost. This was totally unexpected.

When the dance was over, she said "Thank you" and gave me a hug. I went back to my seat. I was flustered to say the least. I just couldn't think straight. I didn't know what to do next.

My thought process was this. She was forward enough to ask me to dance. If she truly liked me, she would have said something more. So, what did I do? I let her go. We both left without meeting again. In fact, the last I saw of her was that last hug goodbye.

In my peaceful times, this memory will eventually find me.

Walking on the beach, looking over an empty field, even having coffee on the porch. I will always come across this replaying in my mind.

This memory is the most beautiful memory I have. Yet, the ending thought is plagued by what I did. I cowered away in the face of love. Not only did I let love slip through my fingers, I literally turned my back on it.

They say that love comes when you're not looking for it. But, I will tell you this. When it DOES come, Be Ready!

Feel the Love on Valentine's Day

Valentine's Day was here again. What was I going to do? I knew it was going to be a big deal and I was stressed about it. I have personally had two relationships end because of events that happened or events that did NOT happen on Valentine's Day. Both of them were in the second year of the relationship, which made me think that this was a pivotal one. Here it was AGAIN. Valentine's Day #2.

Many people want to understate the importance of this day. On a couple's first Valentine's

Day together the feeling is a little laid back. It is effortless. I felt that by the second year into the relationship any issues or doubts were greatly magnified on this day. I felt pressured. As if this day was a test and I had to pass it or else! Sure I bought her a gift, but was this enough?

As I made my way into work, I saw deliverymen at the security desk with flowers and candy. As i walked through the building, I saw about one desk per team that had flowers on top of it. I could see that there were some women that could care less that they did not have gifts delivered. But, there were some that were obviously not happy. It was VERY important to them. I was starting to learn something. It was all about what was important to them but I had a serious problem! I did not even know what she liked on this day of romance.

This was bad! I began to get a little more stressed about this holiday and the pressure it was causing me. I started to blame it on some government plan to keep our economy going. Like some yearly economic stimulus plan to make people go shopping! I was not about to conform to this!! Wait a minute. Whether I liked it or not, this day is in the minds of all women and I had to give her a good experience.

I had to do something to make it special. I had a gift and I picked up a small bunch of flowers on the way to pick her up for dinner. So far, I felt that I was doing well. Then I took her to a place that was nice but not too fancy. We had a nice dinner and she SEEMED happy. In my mind, I was afraid that this was not enough. Searching for anything else to make it more special, I asked her if she would like to go for a walk.

The restaurant was located on a long strip of shops and bars. There were plenty of decorations and lights. They made the area very beautiful for this night. We could hear the bands playing as we walked past the open doors to the bars. Without a thought I took her hand. I realized that it had actually been a few months since I had held her hand.

We reached the end of the block and we turned around to look back into the festive scene. Our hands were now apart. We could have walked back through all of the activity and nice displays. But, the car was also that way so it may have meant that we would have been going back to leave. She took my hand back and led me back in the same direction we had been walking. She had a little smile on her face, so I also smiled and gave her a little kiss as we continued to walk.

I figured out that this day isn't about things or big events. Yes, I learned that I needed to make a few mental notes, but I knew that all she needed was to "Feel the Love" on Valentine's Day.

Made in the USA
Columbia, SC
08 October 2020